SURVEY OF LAW SCHOOL FACULTY & STAFF BEST PRACTICES IN DISTANCE LEGAL EDUCATION

ISBN 978-1-57440-634-4

Contents

THE QUESTIONNAIRE

1. What is the Name of your institution?

    A. Name:
    B. Organization:
    C. Work Title:
    D. Academic Department
    E. Country:
    F. Email Address:

2. Your law school currently enrolls approximately how many students? (Full Time Equivalent)

3. Is your college public or private?

    A. Public
    B. Private

4. What is the approximate annual tuition for your law school prior to any deductions or student aid?

5. Which phrase best describes your law school policy regarding its reaction to the COVID-19 pandemic?

    A. All classes cancelled until further notice
    B. All or most classes moved online until further notice
    C. Increased use of Online Education, restriction on large class sizes or meetings, until further notice
    D. No special measures yet but they are in development

6. Prior to the inception of the pandemic had you ever taught any of the following?

    A. A law class online in a law school
    B. Any class online at any college level
    C. Any college or law school class using blended learning

7. Approximately how much of your work time in the past ten days have you spent on moving classes online or otherwise preparing for online instruction?

8. What kind of instruction or help have you received in setting up your classes online?

9. Are you currently using any of the following in your online instruction?

   A. BlueJean
   B. Zoom
   C. Go To Meeting
   D. Google Hangouts Meet
   E. Skype
   F. Teamviewer
   G. Nearpod
   H. Microsoft Teams
   I. Adobe Connect
   J. UberConference
   K. Other (please specify)

10. Which type of platform do you prefer to deliver most of your course content online?

   A. To deliver course content through a learning management system (such as Canvas, Blackboard many others)
   B. Deliver course content through Twitter, Facebook, YouTube and other video sites and social media
   C. Deliver course contents through Zoom or other group contact and meeting applications
   D. Other (please specify)

11. Which phrase best describes the mixture of real time and video download course delivery in your online education classes?

   A. Deliver my classes in real time over video link, very similar to what it was in the classroom
   B. Mostly delivered in real time in fixed class hours, but with video download/link to lectures for those who cannot attend
   C. Mostly delivered through links or downloads of videos and viewed when convenient for students
   D. Entirely delivered through video downloads links
   E. Other (please specify)

12. For what percentage of the courses that you teach have you created a course site?

13. What have you found most problematic about devising course sites in your learning management system?

14. Have you made lectures or supplemental material available over YouTube, Vimeo or other video sharing site?

    A. Yes
    B. No

15. If you are using Zoom, what can you advise your fellow faculty about its use.

16. Have you established virtual office hours?

    A. Yes
    B. No
    C. No but I am preparing to do this

17. How often do you send a "mass email" to all students in a particular online class?

    A. Daily
    B. Three or four times per week
    C. Once a week
    D. A few times per mont
    E. Monthley
    F. Rarely or never

18. Have you established any of the following for any of your online classes?

    A. Class listserv
    B. Class chat forum
    C. Video downloads
    D. Polls
    E. Course site on Facebook or other social media

19. What do you need the most help with to maximize the effectiveness of your online classes?

20. How satisfied are you with the support that you have received in helping you and your students to move online?

    A. Very satisfied
    B. Satisfied
    C. Neither satisfied nor dissatisfied
    D. Dissatisfied
    E. Very dissatisfied

21. What could your library and IT support services be doing better?

22. What have your library and IT support services done particularly well?

23. How much help have you received from the following in developing and implementing your online courses?

	A great deal of useful help	Some useful help	A little useful help	Help that was not too useful	Have not consulted or been approached by
An Information technology department					
The Library					
An instructional designer					
A distance learning unit or department					
Center for teaching and learning					
Other (please specify)					

24. Has your experience thus far with online education made you think more or less highly of it as an educational tool to be used in law schools after the COVID-19 crisis concludes?

   A. Extremely highly
   B. Very highly
   C. Somewhat highly
   D. Not so highly
   E. Not at all highly

PARTICIPANTS LIST

Boston College Law School
Boyd School of Law UNLV
Buffalo School of Law
Florida International University
Harvard Law School
Hofstra Law School
Loyola Law School Los Angeles
Maryland Law School
Maurice A. Deane School of Law
Mercer University Law School
Rutgers Law School
Temple University Beasley School of Law
Texas Tech University School of Law
The Ohio State University College of Law
Thomas Jefferson SOL
Tulane University
UConn Law School
UIC John Marshall Law School
University of Texas School of Law
University at Buffalo
University of California
University of Connecticut School of Law
University of Denver
University of Florida
University of Florida
University of Mississippi
University of Missouri-Kansas City
University of New Mexico School of Law
University of Notre Dame
University of Pennsylvania
Vanderbilt University
Vermont Law School
Villanova University
Wake Forest School of Law
Widener University
William & Mary Law School

Characteristics of the Sample

U.S. News Law School Ranks

	#
Top 30	13
30 - 65	15
66 - 110	13
More than 110	13
Total	54

Enrollment

	#
Less than 450	14
450 - 579	14
580 -770	15
More than 770	11
Total	54

Is your college public or private?

	#
Public	26
Private	28
Total	54

Tuition, $

	#
Less than 28000	12
28000 - 45999	13
46000 - 56500	13
More than 56500	16
Total	54

SUMMARY OF MAIN FINDINGS

Law Schools Policy on Distance Education

We asked: Which phrase best describes your law school policy regarding its reaction to the COVID-19 pandemic? We gave four possible answers to this multiple- choice question: All classes cancelled until further notice All or most classes moved online until further notice Increased use of Online Education, restriction on large class sizes or meetings, until further notice No special measures yet but they are in development

Overwhelmingly, the majority response was – all or most classes moved online until further notice – given by 96.3% of respondents.

Pervasiveness of Online Legal Education Experience Prior to the Coronavirus

We asked: have you ever taught a law class online in a law school?

Percentage of Work Time Spent in Learning About Online Instruction

We asked: Approximately how much of your work time in the past ten days have you spent on moving classes online or otherwise preparing for online instruction?

The mean was 46.1% and the median 40%; the range was 4% to 100%. The more highly ranked the law school, the lower the percentage of time spent in preparation for online teaching even though experience with online teaching was more common among faculty at lower ranked law schools. For example, top 30 law school faculty spent about 31% of their work time preparing for online teaching vs 57.5% for faculty at institutions ranked over 110. Faculty at public university law schools spent much more of their time preparing for online instruction than did their counterparts in private university law schools. 56.59% vs. 36.48% for private university law schools.

Type of Instruction About Online Instruction Received

We asked: What kind of instruction or help have you received in setting up your classes online?

With a few exceptions most faculty seemed pleased with the help that they were getting, particularly from their IT departments. Zoom training sessions and tutorials were omnipresent; emailed instructions, group chats, webinars, dedicated listservs and group chats, as well as dedicated web pages, video tutorials and one-on-one instruction – all played a welcome role.

Use of Specific Programs and Applications in Online Legal Education

We asked: Are you currently using any of the following in your online instruction?

None used BlueJean. 87.04% are using Zoom; 76.92% of public college faculty but 96.43% of private college law school faculty are using Zoom. None are using Go To Meeting; 3.7% are using Google Hangouts, mostly concentrated among public university law schools. Only 1.85% used Skype. None used TeamViewer or Nearpod. 5.56% used Microsoft Teams, mostly among private college law firms. None used Adobe Connector UberConference. Two programs in common use that were mentioned in a comments section were Panopto and WebEx. WebEx appears to be being used by at least 15% of respondents.

Type of Platform Preferred for Delivering Online Legal Education

We asked: Which type of platform do you prefer to deliver most of your course content online?

We gave four possible answers to this multiple choice question, which were: Other To deliver course content through a learning management system (such as Canvas, Blackboard many others) Deliver course content through Twitter, Facebook, YouTube and other video sites and social media Deliver course contents through Zoom or other group contact and meeting applications

A plurality of 42.59% preferred to deliver course content through Zoom or other group meeting application but 31.48% largely preferred delivery through their course management system such as Canvas or Blackboard and many others. The "Other" option attracted 20.37% of survey participants.

Zoom and related programs was favoured by close to 54% of top 30 law school faculty but only 30.77% of those ranked 110 or over. The larger the law school, the less likely it was to consider options other than Zoom and related programs or the university learning management system. 28.57% of law schools with fewer than 450 students were using one of these "other" options, while only 9.1% of those law schools with more than 770 students was using one of these "other" options. The "other options included systems such as WebEx, Panopto and TWEN.

Synchronous and Asynchronous Delivery

We asked: Which phrase best describes the mixture of real time and video download course delivery in your online education classes?

We gave five possible answers to this multiple-choice question. Other Deliver my classes in real time over video link, very similar to what it was in the classroom Mostly delivered in real time in fixed class hours, but with video download/link to lectures for those who cannot attend Mostly delivered through links or downloads of videos and viewed when convenient for students Entirely delivered through video downloads/links

44.44% delivered their classes in real time, similar to their in-classroom practices. Another 25.93% delivered them in real time at a fixed class hour but also provided links to a video of the lecture for those who could not attend at the defined class hour. Another approximately 15% predominantly delivered their lectures through downloadable video links, viewed by students when convenient for them. Another 12.96% chose the "other" option. Private college law schools were much more likely than public ones to provide links to videos of classroom lectures for students who could not attend at the regular class hours.

Most of those choosing the "other" category likely fit neatly into one of the other categories and most used some mix of real class time and downloadable instruction.

Percentage of Courses with a Course Website

We asked: For what percentage of the courses that you teach have you created a course site?

The mean was 89.58% with little variation for various breakouts and distinctions.

Biggest Problems in Using Course Management System in Distance Learning

We asked: What have you found most problematic about devising course sites in your learning management system?

A hodgepodge of responses, but generally not too any serious complaints.

Use of YouTube, Vimeo and other Video Sites

We asked: have you made lectures or supplemental material available over YouTube, Vimeo or other video sharing site?

29.63% of faculty had done so. This practice was most common among lower ranked and smaller schools. Almost all use of YouTube and other video sharing sites in this respect was by faculty from private universities of whom half used YouTube, Vimeo or other video site.

Advice on Using Zoom

We asked: If you are using Zoom, what can you advise your fellow faculty about its use?

In general Zoom had high satisfaction levels but there were also many suggestions on how to maximize its capabilities.

Percentage of Faculty with Virtual Office Hours

We asked: Have you established virtual office hours?

48.15% of faculty had established virtual office hours and another 7.41% were preparing to do so.

Frequency of Sending Mass Emails to Students in a Class

We asked: How often do you send a "mass email" to all students in a particular online class?

We gave six possible answers to this multiple-choice question; they were: Daily Three or four times per week Once a week A few times per month Monthly Rarely or never

A plurality of 42.59% said three or four times per week and the second most common answer, given by 29.63% of faculty, was 26.93%.

Percentage of Faculty with Class Listserv

We asked: have you established a class listserv for any of your online classes?

About 26% had done so with use greatest at smaller and lower ranked schools; 22.22% had established a chat forum for their classes. 37.04% had established means for downloading videos for their classes; use was greater at private than at public college law schools.

Percentage of Faculty Using Polls in Online Classes

Only 16.67% used polls in their online classes and 1.85% had established a course site on Facebook or other social media site.

Faculty Pressing Needs with Online Teaching

We asked: What do you need the most help with to maximize the effectiveness of your online classes?

A broad range of answers: one mentioned the need for student as well as instructor training and another called for more feedback from students.

Level of Faculty Satisfaction with Institutional Assistance for Distance Legal Education

We asked: How satisfied are you with the support that you have received in helping you and your students to move online?

We gave five possible answers to this multiple-choice question: Very satisfied, Satisfied, Neither satisfied nor dissatisfied, Dissatisfied, Very dissatisfied.

A plurality were very satisfied, given by 51.85% while another 25.93% considered themselves satisfied. Levels of dissatisfaction were highest at the largest law schools and at those in the lowest tuition range.

We asked: What could your library and IT support services be doing better?

In general faculty were quite satisfied.

We asked: What have your library and IT support services done particularly well?

Finesse in Zoom training and quick response times and easy access to help seemed particularly appreciated.

We asked: How much help have you received from the following in developing and implementing your online courses?

We asked separately about the following departments: Information technology department, Library, instructional designer, distance learning unit or department, Center for teaching and learning or Other (please specify).

We gave five possible response to this multiple-choice question; these were: A great deal of useful help Some useful help A little useful help Help that was not too useful Have not consulted or been approached by

For IT departments half of respondents said that they provided a great deal of help with higher ranked and larger law schools presenting the best results for the law school IT departments. For libraries, 37.04% said that they had not consulted nor been approached by the library and 25.93% said that the library had provided a great deal of useful help. The library's role was particularly appreciated by those in smaller institutions which may not have the economies of scale to support large IT support departments.
Instructional designers were not involved at all for 55.66% of faculty. Their help was most useful at private university law schools – 14.29% of faculty at these institutions found that they had provided a great deal of useful help. Overall results were similar for distance learning department and for Centers of Teaching and Learning.

Change in Views of Distance Legal Education as a Result of the Current Experience

We asked: Has your experience thus far with online education made you think more or less highly of it as an educational tool to be used in law schools after the COVID-19 crisis concludes?

In general, the overall opinion of online education has particularly improved at the most highly ranked law schools, where perhaps it was practices less previously. Also, and perhaps for the same reasons, private university law faculty were significantly more likely than public university law faculty to view distance legal education more favourably after this current mass distance education experience.

Table 1.1 Which phrase best describes your law school policy regarding its reaction to the COVID-19 pandemic?

	All classes cancelled until further notice	All or most classes moved online until further notice	Increased use of Online Education, restriction on large class sizes or meetings, until further notice	No special measures yet but they are in development
Entire sample	1.85%	96.30%	1.85%	0.00%

Table 1.2 Which phrase best describes your law school policy regarding its reaction to the COVID-19 pandemic? Broken out by U.S. News Law School Ranks

U.S. News Law School Ranks	All classes cancelled until further notice	All or most classes moved online until further notice	Increased use of Online Education, restriction on large class sizes or meetings, until further notice	No special measures yet but they are in development
Top 30	0.00%	92.31%	7.69%	0.00%
30 - 65	6.67%	93.33%	0.00%	0.00%
66 - 110	0.00%	100.00%	0.00%	0.00%
More than 110	0.00%	100.00%	0.00%	0.00%

Table 1.3 Which phrase best describes your law school policy regarding its reaction to the COVID-19 pandemic? Broken out by enrollment

Enrollment	All classes cancelled until further notice	All or most classes moved online until further notice	Increased use of Online Education, restriction on large class sizes or meetings, until further notice	No special measures yet but they are in development
Less than 450	7.14%	92.86%	0.00%	0.00%
450 - 579	0.00%	92.86%	7.14%	0.00%
580 -770	0.00%	100.00%	0.00%	0.00%
More than 770	0.00%	100.00%	0.00%	0.00%

Table 1.4 Which phrase best describes your law school policy regarding its reaction to the COVID-19 pandemic? Broken out for public and private colleges

Is your college public or private?	All classes cancelled until further notice	All or most classes moved online until further notice	Increased use of Online Education, restriction on large class sizes or meetings, until further notice	No special measures yet but they are in development
Public	3.85%	96.15%	0.00%	0.00%
Private	0.00%	96.43%	3.57%	0.00%

Table 1.5 Which phrase best describes your law school policy regarding its reaction to the COVID-19 pandemic? Broken out by tuition, $

Tuition, $	All classes cancelled until further notice	All or most classes moved online until further notice	Increased use of Online Education, restriction on large class sizes or meetings, until further notice	No special measures yet but they are in development
Less than 28000	0.00%	100.00%	0.00%	0.00%
28000 - 45999	7.69%	92.31%	0.00%	0.00%
46000 - 56500	0.00%	100.00%	0.00%	0.00%
More than 56500	0.00%	93.75%	6.25%	0.00%

Table 2 Prior to the inception of the pandemic had you ever taught any of the following?

Table 2.1.1 Had you ever taught a law class online in a law school?

	No Answer	Yes	No
Entire sample	61.11%	27.78%	11.11%

Table 2.1.2 Had you ever taught a law class online in a law school? Broken out by U.S. News Law School Ranks

U.S. News Law School Ranks	No Answer	Yes	No
Top 30	69.23%	23.08%	7.69%
30 - 65	53.33%	33.33%	13.33%
66 - 110	61.54%	30.77%	7.69%
More than 110	61.54%	23.08%	15.38%

Table 2.1.3 Had you ever taught a law class online in a law school? Broken out by enrollment

Enrollment	No Answer	Yes	No
Less than 450	57.14%	28.57%	14.29%
450 - 579	50.00%	35.71%	14.29%
580 -770	66.67%	26.67%	6.67%
More than 770	72.73%	18.18%	9.09%

Table 2.1.4 Had you ever taught a law class online in a law school? Broken out for public and private colleges

Is your college public or private?	No Answer	Yes	No
Public	69.23%	19.23%	11.54%
Private	53.57%	35.71%	10.71%

Table 2.1.5 Had you ever taught a law class online in a law school? Broken out by tuition, $

Tuition, $	No Answer	Yes	No
Less than 28000	66.67%	25.00%	8.33%
28000 - 45999	61.54%	15.38%	23.08%
46000 - 56500	46.15%	46.15%	7.69%
More than 56500	68.75%	25.00%	6.25%

Table 2.2.1 Had you ever taught any class online at any college level?

	No Answer	Yes	No
Entire sample	61.11%	7.41%	31.48%

Table 2.2.2 Had you ever taught any class online at any college level? Broken out by U.S. News Law School Ranks

U.S. News Law School Ranks	No Answer	Yes	No
Top 30	69.23%	15.38%	15.38%
30 - 65	53.33%	6.67%	40.00%
66 - 110	61.54%	0.00%	38.46%
More than 110	61.54%	7.69%	30.77%

Table 2.2.3 Had you ever taught any class online at any college level? Broken out by enrollment

Enrollment	No Answer	Yes	No
Less than 450	57.14%	0.00%	42.86%
450 - 579	50.00%	21.43%	28.57%
580 -770	66.67%	6.67%	26.67%
More than 770	72.73%	0.00%	27.27%

Table 2.2.4 Had you ever taught any class online at any college level? Broken out for public and private colleges

Is your college public or private?	No Answer	Yes	No
Public	69.23%	0.00%	30.77%
Private	53.57%	14.29%	32.14%

Table 2.2.5 Had you ever taught any class online at any college level? Broken out by tuition, $

Tuition, $	No Answer	Yes	No
Less than 28000	66.67%	0.00%	33.33%
28000 - 45999	61.54%	0.00%	38.46%
46000 - 56500	46.15%	15.38%	38.46%
More than 56500	68.75%	12.50%	18.75%

Table 2.3.1 Had you ever taught any college or law school class using blended learning?

	No Answer	Yes	No
Entire sample	61.11%	24.07%	14.81%

Table 2.3.2 Had you ever taught any college or law school class using blended learning? Broken out by U.S. News Law School Ranks

U.S. News Law School Ranks	No Answer	Yes	No
Top 30	69.23%	23.08%	7.69%
30 - 65	53.33%	26.67%	20.00%
66 - 110	61.54%	23.08%	15.38%
More than 110	61.54%	23.08%	15.38%

Table 2.3.3 Had you ever taught any college or law school class using blended learning? Broken out by enrollment

Enrollment	No Answer	Yes	No
Less than 450	57.14%	21.43%	21.43%
450 - 579	50.00%	35.71%	14.29%
580 -770	66.67%	26.67%	6.67%
More than 770	72.73%	9.09%	18.18%

Table 2.3.4 Had you ever taught any college or law school class using blended learning? Broken out for public and private colleges

Is your college public or private?	No Answer	Yes	No
Public	69.23%	19.23%	11.54%
Private	53.57%	28.57%	17.86%

Table 2.3.5 Had you ever taught any college or law school class using blended learning? Broken out by tuition, $

Tuition, $	No Answer	Yes	No
Less than 28000	66.67%	8.33%	25.00%
28000 - 45999	61.54%	38.46%	0.00%
46000 - 56500	46.15%	23.08%	30.77%
More than 56500	68.75%	25.00%	6.25%

Table 3.1 Approximately how much of your work time in the past ten days have you spent on moving classes online or otherwise preparing for online instruction?

	Mean	Median	Minimum	Maximum
Entire sample	46.10	40.00	4.00	100.00

Table 3.2 Approximately how much of your work time in the past ten days have you spent on moving classes online or otherwise preparing for online instruction? Broken out by U.S. News Law School Ranks

U.S. News Law School Ranks	Mean	Median	Minimum	Maximum
Top 30	30.83	15.00	4.00	95.00
30 - 65	47.67	42.50	4.00	100.00
66 - 110	49.64	50.00	10.00	100.00
More than 110	57.50	75.00	5.00	95.00

Table 3.3 Approximately how much of your work time in the past ten days have you spent on moving classes online or otherwise preparing for online instruction? Broken out by enrollment

Enrollment	Mean	Median	Minimum	Maximum
Less than 450	56.85	75.00	4.00	95.00
450 - 579	25.14	20.00	4.00	60.00
580 -770	42.42	25.00	5.00	100.00
More than 770	59.60	72.50	5.00	100.00

Table 3.4 Approximately how much of your work time in the past ten days have you spent on moving classes online or otherwise preparing for online instruction? Broken out for public and private colleges

Is your college public or private?	Mean	Median	Minimum	Maximum
Public	56.59	72.50	4.00	95.00
Private	36.48	22.50	4.00	100.00

Table 3.5 Approximately how much of your work time in the past ten days have you spent on moving classes online or otherwise preparing for online instruction? Broken out by tuition, $

Tuition, $	Mean	Median	Minimum	Maximum
Less than 28000	60.60	72.50	10.00	95.00
28000 - 45999	54.40	67.50	4.00	95.00
46000 - 56500	41.14	25.00	10.00	100.00
More than 56500	34.53	20.00	4.00	100.00

Broken out by U.S. News Law School Ranks

Top 30

1) Lots of Technology assistance for anyone who needs it.
2) Online training
3) Self-taught and prior experience
4) Zoom training
5) Zoom training
6) BU is advanced in online learning and has many resources. I generally don't need these since I have considerable experience in this area.
7) Tutorials, videos, emails, live IT help during class
8) A lot: videos, manuals & help from my trained faculty assistant
9) Great IT staff with training sessions and personal assistance.
10) A training class at the Law School
11) A group zoom training, emailed instructions, and questions and answers from tech support.
12) Zoom meetings, instructional documents

30 - 65

1) Traiy
2) Extensive training in the relevant software. Our faculty also has a group repository of suggestions for dealing with issues that arise in online learning/teaching.
3) Usual support
4) Online training in Zoom and WebEx
5) Out IT staff has done a phenomenal job in providing first live instruction (before campus closure) and then extensive follow-on Zoom training sessions and has provided a dedicated webpage with helping resources as well as responding via phone and email to individual help requests
6) Demonstrations, dry runs, written instructions
7) Lots of guides/resources/information and support from my administration
8) Lots of emails and resources from the law school administration. College wide resources also.
9) Very little from IT, lots from experienced colleagues.
10) massive help from IT staff and colleagues
11) Our IT Dept. has provided instructional videos.
12) a lot of guidance, webinars
13) Lots of instruction on WEBEX--Great support from Law School IT staff
14) Training classes; individual tutorials with IT staff; private instruction with computer specialist
15) IT department was cooperative and available with tutorials and Q&A availability

66 - 110

1) In person, online, etc. from both law school and University....I have taught asynchronously online so I was helping instruct.
2) Assistance from University's IT and Teaching Excellence departments, as well as outside resources.
3) Online from various law professor blogs and webinars at Zoom
4) My law school offered an instructional session and many emailed resources.
5) training in Zoom, Panopto instruction on different methods for delivering content and managing assessments
6) I have been teaching on line for 18 months. We hired a consultant to help me prepare and we had a series of speakers come over the previous year to prepare the faculty to start teaching online courses
7) IT support
8) Online assistance from the IT dep't
9) Quickly organized training (not great); figured it out as I went
10) We were given instruction by I.T.
11) Advice and technical assistance
12) Instruction on using Zoom and other tools.

More than 110

1) Tutorials from IT staff
2) Excellent help from our IT support personnel anytime I use online instruction, TWEN or internet resources
3) Some IT assistance, memos and group chats with colleagues
4) A one-hour meeting with IT; otherwise self-taught
5) a little bit of online and in-person instruction
6) Online memos; Faculty meeting; Other meetings; Offers of assistance; One-on-One assistance
7) I didn't need any, but tutorials, learning specialist 1 on 1 mtgs and other support was available.
8) links to on-line sources explaining use and best practices
9) Tons of webinars and Zoom meetings
10) Zoom Training and Workshops of Distance Learning
11) IT specialist on staff available by email and phone, extensive online tutorials, faculty sharing experiences
12) A little from the I.T. and technical people over the phone and email

Table 4 Are you currently using any of the following in your online instruction?

Table 4.1.1 Are you currently using BlueJean in your online instruction?

	No Answer	Yes	No
Entire sample	11.11%	0.00%	88.89%

Table 4.2.1 Are you currently using Zoom in your online instruction?

	No Answer	Yes	No
Entire sample	11.11%	87.04%	1.85%

Table 4.2.2 Are you currently using Zoom in your online instruction? Broken out by U.S. News Law School Ranks

U.S. News Law School Ranks	No Answer	Yes	No
Top 30	0.00%	100.00%	0.00%
30 - 65	26.67%	73.33%	0.00%
66 - 110	7.69%	92.31%	0.00%
More than 110	7.69%	84.62%	7.69%

Table 4.2.3 Are you currently using Zoom in your online instruction? Broken out by enrollment

Enrollment	No Answer	Yes	No
Less than 450	14.29%	85.71%	0.00%
450 - 579	14.29%	85.71%	0.00%
580 -770	6.67%	93.33%	0.00%
More than 770	9.09%	81.82%	9.09%

Table 4.2.4 Are you currently using Zoom in your online instruction? Broken out for public and private colleges

Is your college public or private?	No Answer	Yes	No
Public	19.23%	76.92%	3.85%
Private	3.57%	96.43%	0.00%

Table 4.2.5 Are you currently using Zoom in your online instruction? Broken out by tuition, $

Tuition, $	No Answer	Yes	No
Less than 28000	8.33%	91.67%	0.00%
28000 - 45999	23.08%	76.92%	0.00%
46000 - 56500	15.38%	76.92%	7.69%
More than 56500	0.00%	100.00%	0.00%

Table 4.3.1 Are you currently using Go To Meeting in your online instruction?

	No Answer	Yes	No
Entire sample	11.11%	0.00%	88.89%

Table 4.4.1 Are you currently using Google Hangouts Meet in your online instruction?

	No Answer	Yes	No
Entire sample	11.11%	3.70%	85.19%

Table 4.4.2 Are you currently using Google Hangouts Meet in your online instruction? Broken out by U.S. News Law School Ranks

U.S. News Law School Ranks	No Answer	Yes	No
Top 30	0.00%	7.69%	92.31%
30 - 65	26.67%	0.00%	73.33%
66 - 110	7.69%	7.69%	84.62%
More than 110	7.69%	0.00%	92.31%

Table 4.4.3 Are you currently using Google Hangouts Meet in your online instruction? Broken out by enrollment

Enrollment	No Answer	Yes	No
Less than 450	14.29%	0.00%	85.71%
450 - 579	14.29%	7.14%	78.57%
580 -770	6.67%	6.67%	86.67%
More than 770	9.09%	0.00%	90.91%

Table 4.4.4 Are you currently using Google Hangouts Meet in your online instruction? Broken out for public and private colleges

Is your college public or private?	No Answer	Yes	No
Public	19.23%	0.00%	80.77%
Private	3.57%	7.14%	89.29%

Table 4.4.5 Are you currently using Google Hangouts Meet in your online instruction? Broken out by tuition, $

Tuition, $	No Answer	Yes	No
Less than 28000	8.33%	0.00%	91.67%
28000 - 45999	23.08%	0.00%	76.92%
46000 - 56500	15.38%	0.00%	84.62%
More than 56500	0.00%	12.50%	87.50%

Table 4.5.1 Are you currently using Skype in your online instruction?

	No Answer	Yes	No
Entire sample	11.11%	1.85%	87.04%

Table 4.5.2 Are you currently using Skype in your online instruction? Broken out by U.S. News Law School Ranks

U.S. News Law School Ranks	No Answer	Yes	No
Top 30	0.00%	0.00%	100.00%
30 - 65	26.67%	0.00%	73.33%
66 - 110	7.69%	0.00%	92.31%
More than 110	7.69%	7.69%	84.62%

Table 4.5.3 Are you currently using Skype in your online instruction? Broken out by enrollment

Enrollment	No Answer	Yes	No
Less than 450	14.29%	7.14%	78.57%
450 - 579	14.29%	0.00%	85.71%
580 -770	6.67%	0.00%	93.33%
More than 770	9.09%	0.00%	90.91%

Table 4.5.4 Are you currently using Skype in your online instruction? Broken out for public and private colleges

Is your college public or private?	No Answer	Yes	No
Public	19.23%	3.85%	76.92%
Private	3.57%	0.00%	96.43%

Table 4.5.5 Are you currently using Skype in your online instruction? Broken out by tuition, $

Tuition, $	No Answer	Yes	No
Less than 28000	8.33%	8.33%	83.33%
28000 - 45999	23.08%	0.00%	76.92%
46000 - 56500	15.38%	0.00%	84.62%
More than 56500	0.00%	0.00%	100.00%

Table 4.6.1 Are you currently using TeamViewer in your online instruction?

	No Answer	Yes	No
Entire sample	11.11%	0.00%	88.89%

Table 4.7.1 Are you currently using Nearpod in your online instruction?

	No Answer	Yes	No
Entire sample	11.11%	0.00%	88.89%

Table 4.8.1 Are you currently using Microsoft Teams in your online instruction?

	No Answer	Yes	No
Entire sample	11.11%	5.56%	83.33%

Table 4.8.2 Are you currently using Microsoft Teams in your online instruction? Broken out by U.S. News Law School Ranks

U.S. News Law School Ranks	No Answer	Yes	No
Top 30	0.00%	7.69%	92.31%
30 - 65	26.67%	0.00%	73.33%
66 - 110	7.69%	0.00%	92.31%
More than 110	7.69%	15.38%	76.92%

Table 4.8.3 Are you currently using Microsoft Teams in your online instruction? Broken out by enrollment

Enrollment	No Answer	Yes	No
Less than 450	14.29%	0.00%	85.71%
450 - 579	14.29%	14.29%	71.43%
580 -770	6.67%	0.00%	93.33%
More than 770	9.09%	9.09%	81.82%

Table 4.8.4 Are you currently using Microsoft Teams in your online instruction? Broken out for public and private colleges

Is your college public or private?	No Answer	Yes	No
Public	19.23%	3.85%	76.92%
Private	3.57%	7.14%	89.29%

Table 4.8.5 Are you currently using Microsoft Teams in your online instruction? Broken out by tuition, $

Tuition, $	No Answer	Yes	No
Less than 28000	8.33%	0.00%	91.67%
28000 - 45999	23.08%	0.00%	76.92%
46000 - 56500	15.38%	15.38%	69.23%
More than 56500	0.00%	6.25%	93.75%

Table 4.9.1 Are you currently using Adobe Connect in your online instruction?

	No Answer	Yes	No
Entire sample	11.11%	0.00%	88.89%

Table 4.10.1 Are you currently using UberConference in your online instruction?

	No Answer	Yes	No
Entire sample	11.11%	0.00%	88.89%

Other:

1. WebEx teams
2. YouTube, Canvas
3. Web Ex
4. Westlaw's TWEN
5. Canvas
6. WebEx
7. WebEx
8. Panopto
9. Panopto
10. Blackboard
11. Microsoft SharePoint
12. TWEN
13. Canvas
14. mediasite
15. WebEx
16. Blackboard
17. WebEx
18. Panopto

Table 5.1 Which type of platform do you prefer to deliver most of your course content online?

	No Answer	Other	To deliver course content through a learning management system (such as Canvas, Blackboard many others)	Deliver course content through Twitter, Facebook, YouTube and other video sites and social media	Deliver course contents through Zoom or other group contact and meeting applications
Entire sample	5.56%	20.37%	31.48%	0.00%	42.59%

Table 5.2 Which type of platform do you prefer to deliver most of your course content online? Broken out by U.S. News Law School Ranks

U.S. News Law School Ranks	No Answer	Other	To deliver course content through a learning management system (such as Canvas, Blackboard many others)	Deliver course content through Twitter, Facebook, YouTube and other video sites and social media	Deliver course contents through Zoom or other group contact and meeting applications
Top 30	0.00%	7.69%	38.46%	0.00%	53.85%
30 - 65	6.67%	26.67%	26.67%	0.00%	40.00%
66 - 110	7.69%	15.38%	30.77%	0.00%	46.15%
More than 110	7.69%	30.77%	30.77%	0.00%	30.77%

Table 5.3 Which type of platform do you prefer to deliver most of your course content online? Broken out by enrollment

Enrollment	No Answer	Other	To deliver course content through a learning management system (such as Canvas, Blackboard many others)	Deliver course content through Twitter, Facebook, YouTube and other video sites and social media	Deliver course contents through Zoom or other group contact and meeting applications
Less than 450	7.14%	28.57%	14.29%	0.00%	50.00%
450 - 579	0.00%	21.43%	35.71%	0.00%	42.86%
580 -770	13.33%	20.00%	40.00%	0.00%	26.67%
More than 770	0.00%	9.09%	36.36%	0.00%	54.55%

Table 5.4 Which type of platform do you prefer to deliver most of your course content online? Broken out for public and private colleges

Is your college public or private?	No Answer	Other	To deliver course content through a learning management system (such as Canvas, Blackboard many others)	Deliver course content through Twitter, Facebook, YouTube and other video sites and social media	Deliver course contents through Zoom or other group contact and meeting applications
Public	7.69%	23.08%	19.23%	0.00%	50.00%
Private	3.57%	17.86%	42.86%	0.00%	35.71%

Table 5.5 Which type of platform do you prefer to deliver most of your course content online? Broken out by tuition, $

Tuition, $	No Answer	Other	To deliver course content through a learning management system (such as Canvas, Blackboard many others)	Deliver course content through Twitter, Facebook, YouTube and other video sites and social media	Deliver course contents through Zoom or other group contact and meeting applications
Less than 28000	8.33%	8.33%	33.33%	0.00%	50.00%
28000 - 45999	7.69%	30.77%	15.38%	0.00%	46.15%
46000 - 56500	0.00%	30.77%	38.46%	0.00%	30.77%
More than 56500	6.25%	12.50%	37.50%	0.00%	43.75%

Other:

1. A combination, with a learning management system at its center
2. YouTube for video/async and Zoom for live classes
3. Web ex
4. Combination of Zoom + Canvas
5. I don't know enough about what the question is asking to reply intelligently
6. Panopto
7. TWEN
8. mediasite pre-recorded lectures
9. TWEN/WebEx
10. It's the only one I know
11. don't know yet; still working on it

Table 6.1 Which phrase best describes the mixture of real time and video download course delivery in your online education classes?

	No Answer	Other	Deliver my classes in real time over video link, very similar to what it was in the classroom	Mostly delivered in real time in fixed class hours, but with video download/link to lectures for those who cannot attend	Mostly delivered through links or downloads of videos and viewed when convenient for students	Entirely delivered through video downloads/links
Entire sample	1.85%	12.96%	44.44%	25.93%	11.11%	3.70%

Table 6.2 Which phrase best describes the mixture of real time and video download course delivery in your online education classes? Broken out by U.S. News Law School Ranks

U.S. News Law School Ranks	No Answer	Other	Deliver my classes in real time over video link, very similar to what it was in the classroom	Mostly delivered in real time in fixed class hours, but with video download/link to lectures for those who cannot attend	Mostly delivered through links or downloads of videos and viewed when convenient for students	Entirely delivered through video downloads/links
Top 30	0.00%	0.00%	61.54%	30.77%	7.69%	0.00%
30 - 65	0.00%	6.67%	46.67%	26.67%	13.33%	6.67%
66 - 110	0.00%	15.38%	61.54%	7.69%	7.69%	7.69%
More than 110	7.69%	30.77%	7.69%	38.46%	15.38%	0.00%

Table 6.3 Which phrase best describes the mixture of real time and video download course delivery in your online education classes? Broken out by enrollment

Enrollment	No Answer	Other	Deliver my classes in real time over video link, very similar to what it was in the classroom	Mostly delivered in real time in fixed class hours, but with video download/link to lectures for those who cannot attend	Mostly delivered through links or downloads of videos and viewed when convenient for students	Entirely delivered through video downloads/links
Less than 450	7.14%	21.43%	35.71%	14.29%	21.43%	0.00%
450 - 579	0.00%	14.29%	42.86%	35.71%	0.00%	7.14%
580 -770	0.00%	6.67%	53.33%	20.00%	13.33%	6.67%
More than 770	0.00%	9.09%	45.45%	36.36%	9.09%	0.00%

Table 6.4 Which phrase best describes the mixture of real time and video download course delivery in your online education classes? Broken out for public and private colleges

Is your college public or private?	No Answer	Other	Deliver my classes in real time over video link, very similar to what it was in the classroom	Mostly delivered in real time in fixed class hours, but with video download/link to lectures for those who cannot attend	Mostly delivered through links or downloads of videos and viewed when convenient for students	Entirely delivered through video downloads/links
Public	3.85%	15.38%	57.69%	7.69%	15.38%	0.00%
Private	0.00%	10.71%	32.14%	42.86%	7.14%	7.14%

Table 6.5 Which phrase best describes the mixture of real time and video download course delivery in your online education classes? Broken out by tuition, $

Tuition, $	No Answer	Other	Deliver my classes in real time over video link, very similar to what it was in the classroom	Mostly delivered in real time in fixed class hours, but with video download/link to lectures for those who cannot attend	Mostly delivered through links or downloads of videos and viewed when convenient for students	Entirely delivered through video downloads/links
Less than 28000	8.33%	16.67%	50.00%	0.00%	25.00%	0.00%
28000 - 45999	0.00%	23.08%	61.54%	15.38%	0.00%	0.00%
46000 - 56500	0.00%	15.38%	15.38%	46.15%	15.38%	7.69%
More than 56500	0.00%	0.00%	50.00%	37.50%	6.25%	6.25%

Other:

1. Depends on class - for clinic, mostly in real time, for others, online mostly
2. Videos for about 2/3 of class time, 1/3 live
3. Real time class sessions, recorded for those who cannot attend, plus links to video content
4. I do both - one course is asynchronous and the other is synchronous.
5. N/A - as my course is already complete.
6. half via link/download for viewing, half via live Zoom meetings
7. Entirely delivered via downloaded text files and on-line discussion boards

Table 7.1 For what percentage of the courses that you teach have you created a course site?

	Mean	Median	Minimum	Maximum
Entire sample	89.58	100.00	0.00	100.00

Table 7.2 For what percentage of the courses that you teach have you created a course site? Broken out by U.S. News Law School Ranks

U.S. News Law School Ranks	Mean	Median	Minimum	Maximum
Top 30	84.62	100.00	0.00	100.00
30 - 65	92.86	100.00	0.00	100.00
66 - 110	90.00	100.00	0.00	100.00
More than 110	90.91	100.00	0.00	100.00

Table 7.3 For what percentage of the courses that you teach have you created a course site? Broken out by enrollment

Enrollment	Mean	Median	Minimum	Maximum
Less than 450	91.67	100.00	0.00	100.00
450 - 579	92.31	100.00	0.00	100.00
580 -770	91.67	100.00	0.00	100.00
More than 770	81.82	100.00	0.00	100.00

Table 7.4 For what percentage of the courses that you teach have you created a course site? Broken out for public and private colleges

Is your college public or private?	Mean	Median	Minimum	Maximum
Public	90.91	100.00	0.00	100.00
Private	88.46	100.00	0.00	100.00

Table 7.5 For what percentage of the courses that you teach have you created a course site? Broken out by tuition, $

Tuition, $	Mean	Median	Minimum	Maximum
Less than 28000	80.00	100.00	0.00	100.00
28000 - 45999	100.00	100.00	100.00	100.00
46000 - 56500	90.91	100.00	0.00	100.00
More than 56500	85.71	100.00	0.00	100.00

What have you found most problematic about devising course sites in your learning management system? Broken out by U.S. News Law School Ranks

Top 30

1) Uploading video.
2) None
3) The many different systems I use in different institutions
4) Nothing
5) Nothing that I would describe as problematic.
6) Nothing--Canvas does it for me
7) No need or purpose. Columbia already has a Courseworks, which does the same thing.
8) Figuring out how to use it. Once it's figured out, it works quite well.

30 - 65

1) Reliability and internet speed
2) Brightspace does not conveniently print to hard copy.
3) Grading and summary of student online tasks
4) Nothing
5) nothing - we've done this for years
6) None
7) I dislike learning a new on-line interface
8) N/A
9) Canvas is not intuitive or user friendly.
10) N/A
11) Lack of interpersonal interaction in exercises
12) Audio does not always work; getting comfortable with the different options
13) Logistics in setting up the site, I ran a test a week before class and it went well but I still was not comfortable with my ability to maximize WebEx experience for the students

66 - 110

1) CLUNKY
2) None.
3) Lack of assistance from University.
4) Canvas is excellent.
5) Blackboard has some glitches in the grading system...loses comments on tests and papers at times
6) Not applicable
7) TWEN is needlessly time-consuming to set up, cluttered, and not intuitive to use
8) I know the law, not computers
9) Adjusting syllabus in light of new pass/fail grading policy

More than 110

1) There's not the time to do a proper distance learning course to take advantage of Zoom, so this is the next best thing.
2) My relative lack of skills with the internet
3) University or Law School changes in online platforms. I'd prefer to stick with one.
4) It's not intuitive to me and there isn't a lot of capacity in the IT department to tutor me through it.
5) Canvas is not simple to use.
6) No time -- too much work to do right now!
7) Lack of integration with other school systems.
8) Permitting student presentations
9) storage limits for content (1GB)
10) I have never done this before and don't know how

Table 8.1 Have you made lectures or supplemental material available over YouTube, Vimeo or other video sharing site?

	No Answer	Yes	No
Entire sample	3.70%	29.63%	66.67%

Table 8.2 Have you made lectures or supplemental material available over YouTube, Vimeo or other video sharing site? Broken out by U.S. News Law School Ranks

U.S. News Law School Ranks	No Answer	Yes	No
Top 30	0.00%	7.69%	92.31%
30 - 65	0.00%	33.33%	66.67%
66 - 110	7.69%	30.77%	61.54%
More than 110	7.69%	46.15%	46.15%

Table 8.3 Have you made lectures or supplemental material available over YouTube, Vimeo or other video sharing site? Broken out by enrollment

Enrollment	No Answer	Yes	No
Less than 450	14.29%	28.57%	57.14%
450 - 579	0.00%	57.14%	42.86%
580 -770	0.00%	20.00%	80.00%
More than 770	0.00%	9.09%	90.91%

Table 8.4 Have you made lectures or supplemental material available over YouTube, Vimeo or other video sharing site? Broken out for public and private colleges

Is your college public or private?	No Answer	Yes	No
Public	7.69%	7.69%	84.62%
Private	0.00%	50.00%	50.00%

Table 8.5 Have you made lectures or supplemental material available over YouTube, Vimeo or other video sharing site? Broken out by tuition, $

Tuition, $	No Answer	Yes	No
Less than 28000	16.67%	0.00%	83.33%
28000 - 45999	0.00%	38.46%	61.54%
46000 - 56500	0.00%	53.85%	46.15%
More than 56500	0.00%	25.00%	75.00%

If you are using Zoom, what can you advise your fellow faculty about its use? Broken out by U.S. News Law School Ranks

Top 30

1) It's very good, but don't bite off more than you can chew. Start slowly and add functionality when you are comfortable with the basics.
2) Very easy
3) It is a most useful tool. It takes exploration, experimentation and exercise. However, it the best synchronous system I have used for teaching
4) Do it
5) Get an iPad and Apple Pencil to use the whiteboard.
6) Works fine. Have to make sure you don't have waiting room checked, or you will miss students who log on after class starts.
7) Send a memo to the students ahead of time with norms, etiquette and instructions for how to engage in a virtual mode
8) It's fairly easy to manage, even for a Luddite like me
9) Gets better over time- get familiar with new features with each class
10) You need to train faculty on how to record sessions for future viewing, if indeed that can be done.
11) Have the students mute themselves. Pay attention to the background behind you. Pay attention to when people drop off and seek to reconnect.
12) Learn to use it

30 - 65

1) Still learning
2) The biggest problem is maintaining reliable Internet service at home. Two solutions: a mesh net router or using your cell phone's personal hotspot.
3) Zoom allows cool backgrounds, so it appears you're teaching in the xxcking Oval Office Please get out the vote to save us from this idiot
4) Keep it simple. Video and screen share. Mute students first and then call on them individually.
5) Practice with a small number of others (peers, kids, etc.) BEFORE trying to deliver live content to students -- you need to see it as both host and recipient and know what controls are available, etc. and what the views look like on both sides
6) Put a fat book under laptop so that the camera has a better more natural angle
7) Seems to work pretty well and easy to use
8) If you are seeking to annotate the screen, don't use it in conjunction with PowerPoint. A PDF program is much better. Also, the chat feature is helpful to organize class interaction with courses of more than 5 students.
9) It usually works well. It crashed once last week. It also can freeze and/or delay video images, which is pretty disruptive.

66 - 110

1) Learn to play with it in advance!
2) Its features are pretty good, but I wish the polling feature was more advanced.
3) Don't know yet. My first Zoom lecture isn't until next week.
4) I have only begun using it, but it seems to have worked well. It allowed me to share my power point, invite student participation, and receive responses from students using icons. Students who only had phone access were easily able to participate.
5) It's very straightforward, just walk before you run.
6) Good tool
7) Tell Zoom to create a 10-page pamphlet telling the user how to operate they system without subtleties and another for experienced users
8) It's more intuitive than appears at first glance.

More than 110

1) Don't try to use it without asynchronous lectures because it's less efficient, and unless you've thought it through, don't try the (very useful) features it has, for the same reason.
2) No comment, our IT folks handle it for me.
3) If you record classes, save them to the cloud for ease of sharing. Use chat; it's engaging students who used to be quiet
4) Don't replicate the Socratic nonsense. Make a checklist so that you don't mute yourself or forget some other basic thing.
5) I find Zoom very easy to use. Also, the Zoom lecture can be recorded and made available to students who for some reason or the other missed the class session.
6) Have fun with backgrounds, be patient, be willing to change the rhythm of your class engagement.
7) I'm very new to this so nothing at this point
8) It may be best to record yourself and post for students to watch later
9) relatively easy to use, practice before teaching makes it easier
10) not using Zoom

Table 9.1 Have you established virtual office hours?

	No Answer	Yes	No	No but I am preparing to do this
Entire sample	1.85%	48.15%	42.59%	7.41%

Table 9.2 Have you established virtual office hours? Broken out by U.S. News Law School Ranks

U.S. News Law School Ranks	No Answer	Yes	No	No but I am preparing to do this
Top 30	0.00%	38.46%	61.54%	0.00%
30 - 65	0.00%	46.67%	46.67%	6.67%
66 - 110	7.69%	38.46%	46.15%	7.69%
More than 110	0.00%	69.23%	15.38%	15.38%

Table 9.3 Have you established virtual office hours? Broken out by enrollment

Enrollment	No Answer	Yes	No	No but I am preparing to do this
Less than 450	7.14%	35.71%	42.86%	14.29%
450 - 579	0.00%	57.14%	28.57%	14.29%
580 -770	0.00%	53.33%	46.67%	0.00%
More than 770	0.00%	45.45%	54.55%	0.00%

Table 9.4 Have you established virtual office hours? Broken out for public and private colleges

Is your college public or private?	No Answer	Yes	No	No but I am preparing to do this
Public	3.85%	46.15%	38.46%	11.54%
Private	0.00%	50.00%	46.43%	3.57%

Table 9.5 Have you established virtual office hours? Broken out by tuition, $

Tuition, $	No Answer	Yes	No	No but I am preparing to do this
Less than 28000	8.33%	25.00%	58.33%	8.33%
28000 - 45999	0.00%	61.54%	23.08%	15.38%
46000 - 56500	0.00%	76.92%	15.38%	7.69%
More than 56500	0.00%	31.25%	68.75%	0.00%

Table 10.1 How often do you send a "mass email" to all students in a particular online class?

	No Answer	Daily	Three or four times per week	Once a week	A few times per month	Monthly	Rarely or never
Entire sample	1.85%	11.11%	42.59%	29.63%	9.26%	0.00%	5.56%

Table 10.2 How often do you send a "mass email" to all students in a particular online class? Broken out by U.S. News Law School Ranks

U.S. News Law School Ranks	No Answer	Daily	Three or four times per week	Once a week	A few times per month	Monthly	Rarely or never
Top 30	0.00%	15.38%	38.46%	23.08%	15.38%	0.00%	7.69%
30 - 65	0.00%	13.33%	60.00%	20.00%	0.00%	0.00%	6.67%
66 - 110	7.69%	0.00%	38.46%	38.46%	7.69%	0.00%	7.69%
More than 110	0.00%	15.38%	30.77%	38.46%	15.38%	0.00%	0.00%

Table 10.3 How often do you send a "mass email" to all students in a particular online class? Broken out by enrollment

Enrollment	No Answer	Daily	Three or four times per week	Once a week	A few times per month	Monthly	Rarely or never
Less than 450	7.14%	21.43%	35.71%	35.71%	0.00%	0.00%	0.00%
450 - 579	0.00%	14.29%	35.71%	35.71%	14.29%	0.00%	0.00%
580 -770	0.00%	0.00%	53.33%	20.00%	13.33%	0.00%	13.33%
More than 770	0.00%	9.09%	45.45%	27.27%	9.09%	0.00%	9.09%

Table 10.4 How often do you send a "mass email" to all students in a particular online class? Broken out for public and private colleges

Is your college public or private?	No Answer	Daily	Three or four times per week	Once a week	A few times per month	Monthly	Rarely or never
Public	3.85%	15.38%	34.62%	34.62%	3.85%	0.00%	7.69%
Private	0.00%	7.14%	50.00%	25.00%	14.29%	0.00%	3.57%

Table 10.5 How often do you send a "mass email" to all students in a particular online class? Broken out by tuition, $

Tuition, $	No Answer	Daily	Three or four times per week	Once a week	A few times per month	Monthly	Rarely or never
Less than 28000	8.33%	16.67%	25.00%	41.67%	0.00%	0.00%	8.33%
28000 - 45999	0.00%	15.38%	53.85%	23.08%	0.00%	0.00%	7.69%
46000 - 56500	0.00%	15.38%	30.77%	38.46%	15.38%	0.00%	0.00%
More than 56500	0.00%	0.00%	56.25%	18.75%	18.75%	0.00%	6.25%

Table 11 Have you established any of the following for any of your online classes?

Table 11.1.1 Have you established a class listserv for any of your online classes?

	No Answer	Yes	No
Entire sample	33.33%	25.93%	40.74%

Table 11.1.2 Have you established a class listserv for any of your online classes? Broken out by U.S. News Law School Ranks

U.S. News Law School Ranks	No Answer	Yes	No
Top 30	46.15%	15.38%	38.46%
30 - 65	26.67%	20.00%	53.33%
66 - 110	38.46%	23.08%	38.46%
More than 110	23.08%	46.15%	30.77%

Table 11.1.3 Have you established a class listserv for any of your online classes? Broken out by enrollment

Enrollment	No Answer	Yes	No
Less than 450	28.57%	35.71%	35.71%
450 - 579	14.29%	14.29%	71.43%
580 -770	46.67%	26.67%	26.67%
More than 770	45.45%	27.27%	27.27%

Table 11.1.4 Have you established a class listserv for any of your online classes? Broken out for public and private colleges

Is your college public or private?	No Answer	Yes	No
Public	38.46%	26.92%	34.62%
Private	28.57%	25.00%	46.43%

Table 11.1.5 Have you established a class listserv for any of your online classes? Broken out by tuition, $

Tuition, $	No Answer	Yes	No
Less than 28000	50.00%	25.00%	25.00%
28000 - 45999	30.77%	15.38%	53.85%
46000 - 56500	15.38%	46.15%	38.46%
More than 56500	37.50%	18.75%	43.75%

Table 11.2.1 Have you established a class chat forum for any of your online classes?

	No Answer	Yes	No
Entire sample	33.33%	22.22%	44.44%

Table 11.2.2 Have you established a class chat forum for any of your online classes? Broken out by U.S. News Law School Ranks

U.S. News Law School Ranks	No Answer	Yes	No
Top 30	46.15%	15.38%	38.46%
30 - 65	26.67%	26.67%	46.67%
66 - 110	38.46%	23.08%	38.46%
More than 110	23.08%	23.08%	53.85%

Table 11.2.3 Have you established a class chat forum for any of your online classes? Broken out by enrollment

Enrollment	No Answer	Yes	No
Less than 450	28.57%	21.43%	50.00%
450 - 579	14.29%	28.57%	57.14%
580 -770	46.67%	13.33%	40.00%
More than 770	45.45%	27.27%	27.27%

Table 11.2.4 Have you established a class chat forum for any of your online classes? Broken out for public and private colleges

Is your college public or private?	No Answer	Yes	No
Public	38.46%	19.23%	42.31%
Private	28.57%	25.00%	46.43%

Table 11.2.5 Have you established a class chat forum for any of your online classes? Broken out by tuition, $

Tuition, $	No Answer	Yes	No
Less than 28000	50.00%	8.33%	41.67%
28000 - 45999	30.77%	30.77%	38.46%
46000 - 56500	15.38%	30.77%	53.85%
More than 56500	37.50%	18.75%	43.75%

Table 11.3.1 Have you established video downloads for any of your online classes?

	No Answer	Yes	No
Entire sample	33.33%	37.04%	29.63%

Table 11.3.2 Have you established video downloads for any of your online classes? Broken out by U.S. News Law School Ranks

U.S. News Law School Ranks	No Answer	Yes	No
Top 30	46.15%	38.46%	15.38%
30 - 65	26.67%	40.00%	33.33%
66 - 110	38.46%	30.77%	30.77%
More than 110	23.08%	38.46%	38.46%

Table 11.3.3 Have you established video downloads for any of your online classes? Broken out by enrollment

Enrollment	No Answer	Yes	No
Less than 450	28.57%	50.00%	21.43%
450 - 579	14.29%	42.86%	42.86%
580 -770	46.67%	20.00%	33.33%
More than 770	45.45%	36.36%	18.18%

Table 11.3.4 Have you established video downloads for any of your online classes? Broken out for public and private colleges

Is your college public or private?	No Answer	Yes	No
Public	38.46%	30.77%	30.77%
Private	28.57%	42.86%	28.57%

Table 11.3.5 Have you established video downloads for any of your online classes? Broken out by tuition, $

Tuition, $	No Answer	Yes	No
Less than 28000	50.00%	33.33%	16.67%
28000 - 45999	30.77%	46.15%	23.08%
46000 - 56500	15.38%	30.77%	53.85%
More than 56500	37.50%	37.50%	25.00%

Table 11.4.1 Have you used polls for any of your online classes for any of your online classes?

	No Answer	Yes	No
Entire sample	33.33%	16.67%	50.00%

Table 11.4.2 Have you used polls for any of your online classes for any of your online classes? Broken out by U.S. News Law School Ranks

U.S. News Law School Ranks	No Answer	Yes	No
Top 30	46.15%	7.69%	46.15%
30 - 65	26.67%	13.33%	60.00%
66 - 110	38.46%	30.77%	30.77%
More than 110	23.08%	15.38%	61.54%

Table 11.4.3 Have you used polls for any of your online classes for any of your online classes? Broken out by enrollment

Enrollment	No Answer	Yes	No
Less than 450	28.57%	7.14%	64.29%
450 - 579	14.29%	28.57%	57.14%
580 -770	46.67%	13.33%	40.00%
More than 770	45.45%	18.18%	36.36%

Table 11.4.4 Have you used polls for any of your online classes for any of your online classes? Broken out for public and private colleges

Is your college public or private?	No Answer	Yes	No
Public	38.46%	15.38%	46.15%
Private	28.57%	17.86%	53.57%

Table 11.4.5 Have you used polls for any of your online classes for any of your online classes? Broken out by tuition, $

Tuition, $	No Answer	Yes	No
Less than 28000	50.00%	0.00%	50.00%
28000 - 45999	30.77%	23.08%	46.15%
46000 - 56500	15.38%	23.08%	61.54%
More than 56500	37.50%	18.75%	43.75%

Table 11.5.1 Have you established a course site on Facebook or other social media for any of your online classes?

	No Answer	Yes	No
Entire sample	33.33%	1.85%	64.81%

Table 11.5.2 Have you established a course site on Facebook or other social media for any of your online classes? Broken out by U.S. News Law School Ranks

U.S. News Law School Ranks	No Answer	Yes	No
Top 30	46.15%	0.00%	53.85%
30 - 65	26.67%	0.00%	73.33%
66 - 110	38.46%	0.00%	61.54%
More than 110	23.08%	7.69%	69.23%

Table 11.5.3 Have you established a course site on Facebook or other social media for any of your online classes? Broken out by enrollment

Enrollment	No Answer	Yes	No
Less than 450	28.57%	7.14%	64.29%
450 - 579	14.29%	0.00%	85.71%

580 -770	46.67%	0.00%	53.33%
More than 770	45.45%	0.00%	54.55%

Table 11.5.4 Have you established a course site on Facebook or other social media for any of your online classes? Broken out for public and private colleges

Is your college public or private?	No Answer	Yes	No
Public	38.46%	0.00%	61.54%
Private	28.57%	3.57%	67.86%

Table 11.5.5 Have you established a course site on Facebook or other social media for any of your online classes? Broken out by tuition, $

Tuition, $	No Answer	Yes	No
Less than 28000	50.00%	0.00%	50.00%
28000 - 45999	30.77%	7.69%	61.54%
46000 - 56500	15.38%	0.00%	84.62%
More than 56500	37.50%	0.00%	62.50%

What do you need the most help with to maximize the effectiveness of your online classes? Broken out by U.S. News Law School Ranks

Top 30

1) Training
2) Attendance
3) Nothing comes to mind. I make myself completely available thru email, phone, or private Zoom meetings.
4) Mastering Zoom
5) See my earlier comment re recording Zoom sessions for future viewing.
6) How to add outside lecturers to the meeting

30 - 65

1) Practice
2) Setting up and administering final exams. We have always used proctored closed-book exams in live classes. This is expensive to replicate online.
3) A good video conferencing system
4) Better use of live classes
5) I'm good at this point
6) Students having consistent time and Wi-Fi access
7) Feedback from students about what they think about tech and other expectations
8) N/A
9) Zoom
10) back-up support generally; it's all still very new
11) changing screens to show students answering questions

66 - 110

1) Student training!
2) None.
3) Technical assistance on online teaching. I am making it up as I go along.
4) To hear about methods that have proved effective by other professors teaching first year courses.
5) a good 10 page manual
6) computer
7) I have no idea - we're all doing the best we can.
8) More technical IT support

More than 110

1) Time
2) Tech support when I don't have skills with a particular resource I want to bring into the class materials
3) I need a good software platform for video editing
4) To master two or three essential ways of communicating so that they don't get confused and I don't get overwhelmed by the tech options available.
5) Clear explication of the advantages of zoom versus canvas versus Kaltura etc.
6) More preparation time - the students and faculty must have capable technology or Online Learning fails.
7) I don't know yet
8) move time to make them better
9) Everything

Table 12.1 How satisfied are you with the support that you have received in helping you and your students to move online?

	No Answer	Very satisfied	Satisfied	Neither satisfied nor dissatisfied	Dissatisfied	Very dissatisfied
Entire sample	5.56%	51.85%	25.93%	9.26%	7.41%	0.00%

Table 12.2 How satisfied are you with the support that you have received in helping you and your students to move online? Broken out by U.S. News Law School Ranks

U.S. News Law School Ranks	No Answer	Very satisfied	Satisfied	Neither satisfied nor dissatisfied	Dissatisfied	Very dissatisfied
Top 30	0.00%	53.85%	23.08%	15.38%	7.69%	0.00%
30 - 65	6.67%	60.00%	33.33%	0.00%	0.00%	0.00%
66 - 110	7.69%	38.46%	38.46%	7.69%	7.69%	0.00%
More than 110	7.69%	53.85%	7.69%	15.38%	15.38%	0.00%

Table 12.3 How satisfied are you with the support that you have received in helping you and your students to move online? Broken out by enrollment

Enrollment	No Answer	Very satisfied	Satisfied	Neither satisfied nor dissatisfied	Dissatisfied	Very dissatisfied
Less than 450	14.29%	50.00%	14.29%	7.14%	14.29%	0.00%
450 - 579	0.00%	50.00%	50.00%	0.00%	0.00%	0.00%
580 -770	6.67%	60.00%	20.00%	13.33%	0.00%	0.00%
More than 770	0.00%	45.45%	18.18%	18.18%	18.18%	0.00%

Table 12.4 How satisfied are you with the support that you have received in helping you and your students to move online? Broken out for public and private colleges

Is your college public or private?	No Answer	Very satisfied	Satisfied	Neither satisfied nor dissatisfied	Dissatisfied	Very dissatisfied
Public	7.69%	46.15%	26.92%	11.54%	7.69%	0.00%
Private	3.57%	57.14%	25.00%	7.14%	7.14%	0.00%

Table 12.5 How satisfied are you with the support that you have received in helping you and your students to move online? Broken out by tuition, $

Tuition, $	No Answer	Very satisfied	Satisfied	Neither satisfied nor dissatisfied	Dissatisfied	Very dissatisfied
Less than 28000	16.67%	41.67%	16.67%	16.67%	8.33%	0.00%
28000 - 45999	0.00%	61.54%	23.08%	7.69%	7.69%	0.00%
46000 - 56500	0.00%	30.77%	53.85%	7.69%	7.69%	0.00%
More than 56500	6.25%	68.75%	12.50%	6.25%	6.25%	0.00%

What could your library and IT support services be doing better? Broken out by U.S. News Law School Ranks

Top 30

1) Nothing
2) Nothing.
3) Nothing
4) n/a

30 - 65

1) Yes
2) Very little. We have spectacular support.
3) They're doing fine
4) Nothing
5) Nothing
6) None
7) Providing student feedback
8) N/A
9) cleaer instructions
10) They have been wonderful!

66 - 110

1) NOTHING - we had to do it so fast they worked miracles
2) Continue to offer webinars and resources for variety of online learning services
3) With only one IT person at the Law School, he is there to put out fires, not prov de support.
4) Nothing.
5) Not applicable
6) Eliminate the countless duplicative and superfluous emails being sent by everybody at the law school ostensibly related to online instruction.
7) We need more IT people. They are overworked and stressed.
8) they're great - if it's not broken, don't fix it
9) Publish list of problems encountered by other faculty and either fixes for the problem or advice to contact IT department

More than 110

1) With more time, yes.
2) No thoughts on this.
3) Our IT folks are amazing
4) More time, better communication
5) Think, first, about what I need as a teacher rather than impose solutions on me.
6) They've been great - the lack of lifecycle funding for technology (laptop replacement) is causing the main issues we are having.
7) We just started this, so I don't know at this point.
8) Someone over my shoulder at all times.
9) I can't even begin to answer that

What have your library and IT support services done particularly well? Broken out by U.S. News Law School Ranks

Top 30

1) Everything, given the givens.
2) Zoom training
3) In person help
4) Set up the Zoom and Blackboard resources for intuitive access and utilization.
5) Everything
6) n/a
7) IT was very responsive when I had difficulties establishing password protection.

30 - 65

1) Response time
2) Training and being available when things go wrong.
3) Stayed at home
4) Answered individual questions
5) Training!!
6) Explain
7) Been available to help
8) N/A
9) responsiveness to individual needs
10) available any time to help solve problems
11) Immediate response; great infrastructure and teaching online programs and VPN
12) Patience; explained very clearly; non-judgmental

66 - 110

1) Almost everything...and they are ESPECIALLY patient!
2) Make themselves available, offer resources and support.
3) Timely ordered Logitech webcams.
4) They have shared extensive resources.
5) They have been on top of everything
6) All support
7) They've been helpful and timely in response to emails
8) giving us tips and instructional videos.
9) Respond to phone calls asking for help and scheduling instructional classes

More than 110

1) Given the circumstances, yes.
2) Helping older professors with relatively less skill with IT/computer issues.
3) Our Library/IT staff has reached out to students and actively solved problems; they are even checking out refurbished iPhone for use as portable Wi-Fi hot spots, and they have loaner tablets and computers for students in need. 100% of my students have the equipment and software they need to access classes online.
4) Library has made books available--appreciated
5) My library has not been involved. IT has done a good job in being enthusiastic.
6) Tutorials, online meetings, one on one "service calls"
7) Same.
8) Get material I request
9) Training and locating resources (webcams, etc.)
10) availability to answer questions, set up technology
11) express sympathy

Table 13 How much help have you received from the following in developing and implementing your online courses?

Table 13.1.1 How much help have you received from the Information technology department in developing and implementing your online courses?

	No Answer	A great deal of useful help	Some useful help	A little useful help	Help that was not too useful	Have not consulted or been approached by
Entire sample	9.26%	50.00%	25.93%	7.41%	1.85%	5.56%

Table 13.1.2 How much help have you received from the Information technology department in developing and implementing your online courses? Broken out by U.S. News Law School Ranks

U.S. News Law School Ranks	No Answer	A great deal of useful help	Some useful help	A little useful help	Help that was not too useful	Have not consulted or been approached by
Top 30	0.00%	53.85%	38.46%	7.69%	0.00%	0.00%
30 - 65	6.67%	60.00%	6.67%	13.33%	0.00%	13.33%
66 - 110	7.69%	38.46%	46.15%	7.69%	0.00%	0.00%
More than 110	23.08%	46.15%	15.38%	0.00%	7.69%	7.69%

Table 13.1.3 How much help have you received from the Information technology department in developing and implementing your online courses? Broken out by enrollment

Enrollment	No Answer	A great deal of useful help	Some useful help	A little useful help	Help that was not too useful	Have not consulted or been approached by
Less than 450	14.29%	42.86%	28.57%	7.14%	0.00%	7.14%
450 - 579	7.14%	50.00%	21.43%	14.29%	0.00%	7.14%
580 -770	13.33%	46.67%	26.67%	6.67%	0.00%	6.67%
More than 770	0.00%	63.64%	27.27%	0.00%	9.09%	0.00%

Table 13.1.4 How much help have you received from the Information technology department in developing and implementing your online courses? Broken out for public and private colleges

Is your college public or private?	No Answer	A great deal of useful help	Some useful help	A little useful help	Help that was not too useful	Have not consulted or been approached by
Public	11.54%	46.15%	26.92%	3.85%	3.85%	7.69%
Private	7.14%	53.57%	25.00%	10.71%	0.00%	3.57%

Table 13.1.5 How much help have you received from the Information technology department in developing and implementing your online courses? Broken out by tuition, $

Tuition, $	No Answer	A great deal of useful help	Some useful help	A little useful help	Help that was not too useful	Have not consulted or been approached by
Less than 28000	16.67%	33.33%	41.67%	8.33%	0.00%	0.00%
28000 - 45999	0.00%	61.54%	23.08%	0.00%	0.00%	15.38%
46000 - 56500	15.38%	46.15%	7.69%	15.38%	7.69%	7.69%
More than 56500	6.25%	56.25%	31.25%	6.25%	0.00%	0.00%

Table 13.2.1 How much help have you received from the Library in developing and implementing your online courses?

	No Answer	A great deal of useful help	Some useful help	A little useful help	Help that was not too useful	Have not consulted or been approached by
Entire sample	12.96%	25.93%	18.52%	5.56%	0.00%	37.04%

Table 13.2.2 How much help have you received from the Library in developing and implementing your online courses? Broken out by U.S. News Law School Ranks

U.S. News Law School Ranks	No Answer	A great deal of useful help	Some useful help	A little useful help	Help that was not too useful	Have not consulted or been approached by
Top 30	7.69%	7.69%	0.00%	7.69%	0.00%	76.92%
30 - 65	13.33%	40.00%	13.33%	6.67%	0.00%	26.67%
66 - 110	7.69%	15.38%	30.77%	7.69%	0.00%	38.46%
More than 110	23.08%	38.46%	30.77%	0.00%	0.00%	7.69%

Table 13.2.3 How much help have you received from the Library in developing and implementing your online courses? Broken out by enrollment

Enrollment	No Answer	A great deal of useful help	Some useful help	A little useful help	Help that was not too useful	Have not consulted or been approached by
Less than 450	14.29%	28.57%	28.57%	7.14%	0.00%	21.43%
450 - 579	14.29%	28.57%	21.43%	7.14%	0.00%	28.57%
580 -770	13.33%	26.67%	6.67%	6.67%	0.00%	46.67%
More than 770	9.09%	18.18%	18.18%	0.00%	0.00%	54.55%

Table 13.2.4 How much help have you received from the Library in developing and implementing your online courses? Broken out for public and private colleges

Is your college public or private?	No Answer	A great deal of useful help	Some useful help	A little useful help	Help that was not too useful	Have not consulted or been approached by
Public	19.23%	26.92%	23.08%	3.85%	0.00%	26.92%
Private	7.14%	25.00%	14.29%	7.14%	0.00%	46.43%

Table 13.2.5 How much help have you received from the Library in developing and implementing your online courses? Broken out by tuition, $

Tuition, $	No Answer	A great deal of useful help	Some useful help	A little useful help	Help that was not too useful	Have not consulted or been approached by
Less than 28000	25.00%	25.00%	16.67%	8.33%	0.00%	25.00%
28000 - 45999	7.69%	38.46%	30.77%	0.00%	0.00%	23.08%
46000 - 56500	15.38%	15.38%	23.08%	7.69%	0.00%	38.46%
More than 56500	6.25%	25.00%	6.25%	6.25%	0.00%	56.25%

Table 13.3.1 How much help have you received from the instructional designer in developing and implementing your online courses?

	No Answer	A great deal of useful help	Some useful help	A little useful help	Help that was not too useful	Have not consulted or been approached by
Entire sample	14.81%	9.26%	11.11%	9.26%	0.00%	55.56%

Table 13.3.2 How much help have you received from the instructional designer in developing and implementing your online courses? Broken out by U.S. News Law School Ranks

U.S. News Law School Ranks	No Answer	A great deal of useful help	Some useful help	A little useful help	Help that was not too useful	Have not consulted or been approached by
Top 30	0.00%	7.69%	15.38%	15.38%	0.00%	61.54%
30 - 65	26.67%	20.00%	6.67%	6.67%	0.00%	40.00%
66 - 110	7.69%	7.69%	15.38%	0.00%	0.00%	69.23%
More than 110	23.08%	0.00%	7.69%	15.38%	0.00%	53.85%

Table 13.3.3 How much help have you received from the instructional designer in developing and implementing your online courses? Broken out by enrollment

Enrollment	No Answer	A great deal of useful help	Some useful help	A little useful help	Help that was not too useful	Have not consulted or been approached by
Less than 450	14.29%	7.14%	7.14%	14.29%	0.00%	57.14%
450 - 579	21.43%	7.14%	21.43%	0.00%	0.00%	50.00%
580 -770	20.00%	6.67%	0.00%	13.33%	0.00%	60.00%
More than 770	0.00%	18.18%	18.18%	9.09%	0.00%	54.55%

Table 13.3.4 How much help have you received from the instructional designer in developing and implementing your online courses? Broken out for public and private colleges

Is your college public or private?	No Answer	A great deal of useful help	Some useful help	A little useful help	Help that was not too useful	Have not consulted or been approached by
Public	23.08%	3.85%	15.38%	11.54%	0.00%	46.15%
Private	7.14%	14.29%	7.14%	7.14%	0.00%	64.29%

Table 13.3.5 How much help have you received from the instructional designer in developing and implementing your online courses? Broken out by tuition, $

Tuition, $	No Answer	A great deal of useful help	Some useful help	A little useful help	Help that was not too useful	Have not consulted or been approached by
Less than 28000	16.67%	0.00%	16.67%	16.67%	0.00%	50.00%
28000 - 45999	15.38%	7.69%	7.69%	7.69%	0.00%	61.54%
46000 - 56500	23.08%	15.38%	23.08%	0.00%	0.00%	38.46%
More than 56500	6.25%	12.50%	0.00%	12.50%	0.00%	68.75%

Table 13.4.1 How much help have you received from the distance learning unit or department in developing and implementing your online courses?

	No Answer	A great deal of useful help	Some useful help	A little useful help	Help that was not too useful	Have not consulted or been approached by
Entire sample	12.96%	9.26%	7.41%	12.96%	1.85%	55.56%

Table 13.4.2 How much help have you received from the distance learning unit or department in developing and implementing your online courses? Broken out by U.S. News Law School Ranks

U.S. News Law School Ranks	No Answer	A great deal of useful help	Some useful help	A little useful help	Help that was not too useful	Have not consulted or been approached by
Top 30	0.00%	15.38%	15.38%	7.69%	0.00%	61.54%
30 - 65	20.00%	13.33%	6.67%	13.33%	0.00%	46.67%
66 - 110	7.69%	0.00%	0.00%	15.38%	0.00%	76.92%
More than 110	23.08%	7.69%	7.69%	15.38%	7.69%	38.46%

Table 13.4.3 How much help have you received from the distance learning unit or department in developing and implementing your online courses? Broken out by enrollment

Enrollment	No Answer	A great deal of useful help	Some useful help	A little useful help	Help that was not too useful	Have not consulted or been approached by
Less than 450	14.29%	7.14%	7.14%	7.14%	7.14%	57.14%
450 - 579	14.29%	14.29%	7.14%	28.57%	0.00%	35.71%
580 -770	20.00%	13.33%	0.00%	6.67%	0.00%	60.00%
More than 770	0.00%	0.00%	18.18%	9.09%	0.00%	72.73%

Table 13.4.4 How much help have you received from the distance learning unit or department in developing and implementing your online courses? Broken out for public and private colleges

Is your college public or private?	No Answer	A great deal of useful help	Some useful help	A little useful help	Help that was not too useful	Have not consulted or been approached by
Public	19.23%	7.69%	7.69%	7.69%	3.85%	53.85%
Private	7.14%	10.71%	7.14%	17.86%	0.00%	57.14%

Table 13.4.5 How much help have you received from the distance learning unit or department in developing and implementing your online courses? Broken out by tuition, $

Tuition, $	No Answer	A great deal of useful help	Some useful help	A little useful help	Help that was not too useful	Have not consulted or been approached by
Less than 28000	16.67%	0.00%	8.33%	8.33%	8.33%	58.33%
28000 - 45999	15.38%	15.38%	7.69%	15.38%	0.00%	46.15%
46000 - 56500	15.38%	7.69%	7.69%	23.08%	0.00%	46.15%
More than 56500	6.25%	12.50%	6.25%	6.25%	0.00%	68.75%

Table 13.5.1 How much help have you received from the Center for teaching and learning in developing and implementing your online courses?

	No Answer	A great deal of useful help	Some useful help	A little useful help	Help that was not too useful	Have not consulted or been approached by
Entire sample	12.96%	5.56%	16.67%	14.81%	1.85%	48.15%

Table 13.5.2 How much help have you received from the Center for teaching and learning in developing and implementing your online courses? Broken out by U.S. News Law School Ranks

U.S. News Law School Ranks	No Answer	A great deal of useful help	Some useful help	A little useful help	Help that was not too useful	Have not consulted or been approached by
Top 30	0.00%	0.00%	15.38%	23.08%	0.00%	61.54%
30 - 65	20.00%	6.67%	13.33%	6.67%	6.67%	46.67%
66 - 110	7.69%	0.00%	23.08%	7.69%	0.00%	61.54%
More than 110	23.08%	15.38%	15.38%	23.08%	0.00%	23.08%

Table 13.5.3 How much help have you received from the Center for teaching and learning in developing and implementing your online courses? Broken out by enrollment

Enrollment	No Answer	A great deal of useful help	Some useful help	A little useful help	Help that was not too useful	Have not consulted or been approached by
Less than 450	21.43%	0.00%	21.43%	14.29%	0.00%	42.86%
450 - 579	14.29%	14.29%	21.43%	21.43%	7.14%	21.43%
580 -770	13.33%	6.67%	13.33%	13.33%	0.00%	53.33%
More than 770	0.00%	0.00%	9.09%	9.09%	0.00%	81.82%

Table 13.5.4 How much help have you received from the Center for teaching and learning in developing and implementing your online courses? Broken out for public and private colleges

Is your college public or private?	No Answer	A great deal of useful help	Some useful help	A little useful help	Help that was not too useful	Have not consulted or been approached by
Public	19.23%	3.85%	19.23%	7.69%	0.00%	50.00%
Private	7.14%	7.14%	14.29%	21.43%	3.57%	46.43%

Table 13.5.5 How much help have you received from the Center for teaching and learning in developing and implementing your online courses? Broken out by tuition, $

Tuition, $	No Answer	A great deal of useful help	Some useful help	A little useful help	Help that was not too useful	Have not consulted or been approached by
Less than 28000	16.67%	0.00%	8.33%	16.67%	0.00%	58.33%
28000 - 45999	15.38%	7.69%	38.46%	7.69%	0.00%	30.77%
46000 - 56500	15.38%	15.38%	15.38%	15.38%	7.69%	30.77%
More than 56500	6.25%	0.00%	6.25%	18.75%	0.00%	68.75%

Other:

1. I have done this before so the trainings were for the novice
2. Peers
3. Colleagues' advice based on experience — a lot.
4. I did this myself b/c I could. I didn't need assistance to make it happen.
5. Dean, Assistant Dean, Faculty Assistant
6. grandson
7. Faculty to Faculty on-line conversations
8. colleagues

Table 14.1 Has your experience thus far with online education made you think more or less highly of it as an educational tool to be used in law schools after the COVID-19 crisis concludes?

	No Answer	Extremely highly	Very highly	Somewhat highly	Not so highly	Not at all highly
Entire sample	5.56%	14.81%	22.22%	29.63%	16.67%	11.11%

Table 14.2 Has your experience thus far with online education made you think more or less highly of it as an educational tool to be used in law schools after the COVID-19 crisis concludes? Broken out by U.S. News Law School Ranks

U.S. News Law School Ranks	No Answer	Extremely highly	Very highly	Somewhat highly	Not so highly	Not at all highly
Top 30	0.00%	15.38%	23.08%	38.46%	15.38%	7.69%
30 - 65	6.67%	13.33%	26.67%	20.00%	20.00%	13.33%
66 - 110	7.69%	23.08%	0.00%	23.08%	30.77%	15.38%
More than 110	7.69%	7.69%	38.46%	38.46%	0.00%	7.69%

Table 14.3 Has your experience thus far with online education made you think more or less highly of it as an educational tool to be used in law schools after the COVID-19 crisis concludes? Broken out by enrollment

Enrollment	No Answer	Extremely highly	Very highly	Somewhat highly	Not so highly	Not at all highly
Less than 450	14.29%	7.14%	28.57%	28.57%	21.43%	0.00%
450 - 579	0.00%	14.29%	28.57%	21.43%	28.57%	7.14%
580 -770	6.67%	26.67%	13.33%	13.33%	13.33%	26.67%
More than 770	0.00%	9.09%	18.18%	63.64%	0.00%	9.09%

Table 14.4 Has your experience thus far with online education made you think more or less highly of it as an educational tool to be used in law schools after the COVID-19 crisis concludes? Broken out for public and private colleges

Is your college public or private?	No Answer	Extremely highly	Very highly	Somewhat highly	Not so highly	Not at all highly
Public	7.69%	7.69%	19.23%	30.77%	23.08%	11.54%
Private	3.57%	21.43%	25.00%	28.57%	10.71%	10.71%

Table 14.5 Has your experience thus far with online education made you think more or less highly of it as an educational tool to be used in law schools after the COVID-19 crisis concludes? Broken out by tuition, $

Tuition, $	No Answer	Extremely highly	Very highly	Somewhat highly	Not so highly	Not at all highly
Less than 28000	16.67%	0.00%	16.67%	41.67%	16.67%	8.33%
28000 - 45999	0.00%	15.38%	23.08%	38.46%	15.38%	7.69%
46000 - 56500	0.00%	15.38%	30.77%	15.38%	23.08%	15.38%
More than 56500	6.25%	25.00%	18.75%	25.00%	12.50%	12.50%

Made in United States
Orlando, FL
04 November 2026

90200448R00046